The Rise of Anime and Manga

THE MAKING OF ANIME AND MANGA

From Zodiac Animal Shifters to Demon Slayers

MARI BOLTE

TWENTY-FIRST CENTURY BOOKS / MINNEAPOLIS

When I wake up in the morning, I count my blessings that I'm not as busy as a mangaka but am thankful they exist so I have something to read at the end of the day.

Twenty-First Century Books™
An imprint of Lerner Publishing Group, Inc.
241 First Avenue North
Minneapolis, MN 55401 USA

For reading levels and more information, look up this title at www.lernerbooks.com.

Main body text set in Bembo Std Regular.
Typeface provided by Monotype Typography.

Library of Congress Cataloging-in-Publication Data

Names: Bolte, Mari author
Title: *The making of anime and manga : from zodiac animal shifters to demon slayers* / Mari Bolte.
Description: Minneapolis : Twenty-First Century Books, 2026. | Series: The rise of anime and manga | Includes bibliographical references and index. | Audience: Ages 11–18 | Audience: Grades 7–9 | Summary: "Lots of people work together to bring anime and manga to life! Learn about the behind-the-scenes work that goes into creating and polishing anime and manga from the publishers to studios, directors, and voice actors"—Provided by publisher.
Identifiers: LCCN 2025011231 (print) | LCCN 2025011232 (ebook) | ISBN 9798765662755 library binding | ISBN 9798348029654 paperback | ISBN 9798348000448 epub
Subjects: LCSH: Animated television programs—Production and direction—Japan—Juvenile literature | Animated films—Production and direction—Japan—Juvenile literature | Manga (Comic books)—Authorship—Juvenile literature
Classification: LCC PN1992.8.A59 B65 2026 (print) | LCC PN1992.8.A59 (ebook) | DDC 791.45/34—dc23/eng/20250527

LC record available at https://lccn.loc.gov/2025011231
LC ebook record available at https://lccn.loc.gov/2025011232

Manufactured in the United States of America
1 – CG – 12/15/25

CONTENTS

INTRODUCTION

Anime and manga have been entertaining people around the world for decades. Whether you're looking for the latest volume of your favorite manga on the bookstore shelf or flipping through a streaming service to find something new, there's always something to read, watch, and enjoy.

People can experience anime and manga in many ways. They can read or watch it in the original Japanese or translated into their own language. They can download chapters or episodes over the internet without ever leaving their home. People can even spot popular characters in movie theaters, floating in the Macy's Thanksgiving Day Parade, and eating Kentucky Fried Chicken and McDonald's in advertisements.

A lot goes into creating anime and manga. Most manga creators are both the writer and the illustrator. It can take between five and fifteen hours of work to complete just a single manga page. Meanwhile, animating a single episode

Fans around the world enjoy manga for its detail, emotion, and sense of adventure.

of anime can take eight weeks or longer. But none of that includes mapping out the story, adding details, recording sound, or getting it printed. It's an intensive process and requires all hands on deck to get it done. Even minute details need to be hashed out. "When I'm working on the graphic novel [tankobon] version, I have a lot of meetings with the designer—more than you'd think," *Assassination Classroom* author Yusei Matsui wrote. "The main reason for these meetings is to make fine adjustments to the cover color. . . . Even the slightest difference in color will change the impression the cover makes on a reader."

CHAPTER ONE

Previously On . . .

Anime productions often have a whole team dedicated to working on a series. From directors to key animators to background artists, creating just a single episode can take anywhere from a few weeks to a few months. To understand how modern Japanese animation came to be, let's take a look at the first film technologies.

The First Film Technologies

In the mid-eighteenth century, Dutch traders introduced a simple image projector called a magic lantern to Japan. These were handheld lanterns. People used light to project an image from a transparent plate onto a wall or screen so that it appeared larger than it actually was.

Japan eventually adapted magic lanterns into a form of entertainment called utsushi-e. Pictures were printed onto rice paper or glass. Then, multiple lanterns projected the pictures onto walls, ceilings, or even other people to tell a story. To heighten the drama, storytellers added color,

Magic lanterns were loaded with images on transparent plates called slides. The slides were actually loaded upside down, and the magic lantern projected them right side up.

lighting effects, and music. Even better, by projecting two slides at once—one still slide in the back of the magic lantern and one mobile slide in the front—a viewer could be tricked into believing the picture was in motion. But the ability to capture and show motion in film hadn't been invented yet.

In 1891, American inventor Thomas Edison developed the kinetoscope. Edison had been inspired by French scientist Étienne-Jules Marey and his device that captured consecutive images on a long piece of film—the result being a motion picture—and Edison incorporated this technology into the kinetoscope. The machine contained a strip of film with forty-six frames. These frames then moved behind a lens and a light source. Viewers saw a fraction of each frame through a peephole, which gave the illusion of movement.

In 1896, the first public movie showing in Japan was held in Kobe. The next year, Japan witnessed the cinematograph in action. This camera and projector apparatus was invented by the Lumière brothers, famous pioneers in early photography. The device was smaller than the kinetoscope and not reliant on electricity. Films were several minutes long and accompanied by music. Narrators introduced the projectors at viewings and explained how they worked. Then, they would give the movie's plot. No permanent movie theaters existed at this time. Instead, crews showed movies for around a week and then moved to another location.

This magic lantern slide depicts a scene from *The Tale of Genji.*

Japan began making their own movies in 1899. But the oldest surviving animation only dates back to 1917. The films were less than five minutes long. Originally, these films were drawn with chalk. Each frame would be recorded, and then the animator would erase the chalk drawing and add new lines. Not many of these early films survive today.

Animation's Evolution

Cel animation began in Japan in the 1930s and became the popular go-to for studios for decades. This was a style of animation that required animators to hand-draw onto transparent celluloid sheets called cels. To create the illusion of movement, animators would draw a character on a cel sheet, then draw the character again on another cel sheet so it differed just slightly from the one before it. After having amassed enough of these cel sheets, a person could flip through them, and it would look like the character was moving.

Oftentimes, the cel sheet would begin with just a pencil sketch with instructions of where to color and shade. Then the cel sheet would pass onto the next animator, who would fill in the colors. Cel sheets were often placed on painted backgrounds and then photographed by a camera. Ink lines were thick, and color was bold and blocky.

But cel animation had a caveat. It was time-consuming, and often required animators to redraw full frames. As more things around the world started to become digital, so did animation. And Japan began combining the two mediums.

The Dull Sword is the oldest surviving anime. The four-minute-long film dates back to 1917.

Three Pieces of History

One of the first anime that aired across Japan was the 1960 short film *Three Tales*. It had three parts. Each part adapted a fairy tale written by children's book authors Hirosuke Hamada, Kenji Miyazawa, and Mimei Ogawa. The film used cutout characters to create stop-motion animation that simulated movement. Atypical compared to most modern productions, the directors and animators for this project were all children's book illustrators.

Drawing Goes Digital

In the mid-1990s, the industry shifted toward digital animation. The first anime to try computer-generated imagery (CGI) was *Bit the Cupid* in 1995. It used digital paint and ink as well as CGI. *Cupid*'s creator Susumu Matsushita typically worked on video games and magazine covers, so his airbrush style fit the experimental technique. But it was the 1995 movie adaptation of *Ghost in the Shell* that would test the limits of technology and animation.

Directed by Mamoru Oshii, *Ghost in the Shell* showcased digital animation's advancements. It used digitally generated animation (DGA) that combined traditional cel animation, motion capture with computer images, and audio entered as digital data, blending them to add realism to the futuristic technology-led world. As each component was added, it was turned into digital data that software programs could then read. Movement captured through motion capture would show up on a computer screen as a 3D model. When animation was added to the model, the character appeared to move just like a real person. Hand-drawn cel animation was layered over digital cel animation, giving backgrounds depth and movement. Even light was tweaked, with animators paying special attention to realistic lighting sources and natural shadows. Because *Ghost in the Shell*'s author, Shirow Masamune, had a sizable global following, the film received overseas funding, which meant the production team was able to dedicate a big budget toward its impressive computer animation.

In 2017, *Ghost in the Shell* became a live-action movie. Many viewers praised its visual effects but critiqued its casting and plot.

CGI Anime

The first anime to be fully animated using CGI was the 2000 sci-fi comedy drama *A.Li.Ce.* The film included well-staged action sequences and made effective use of its CGI. Many critics, however, pointed out that characters' facial movements had limited range, impeding their ability to properly convey emotions to the audience. But that didn't stop animators from improving on the technology.

Studios got to work. In 2004, Eiji Inomoto, who had worked on *Ghost in the Shell: Stand Alone Complex* (the sequel to *Ghost in the Shell*), founded Studio Orange. The studio quickly made a name for themselves in 3DCG animation. Not only did they begin producing their own 3DCG projects, they did 3D work for other studios. In 2017, they released the show *Land of the Lustrous.* The studio combined hand-drawn 2D animation with computer-generated 3D animation to create vibrant, glassy animation with smooth movements. Their next big project, *Beastars*, an adult show about anthropomorphic animals, used facial capture software to make character expressions look more lifelike and move in realistic ways. In other projects, Studio Orange has used Unreal Engine, a 3D creation tool used by video game developers including Epic, which makes games such as *Fortnite* and *Rocket League.*

Some people feel that 3DCG animation is a betrayal of the source material. Others like that old favorites are given a fresh start. *Trigun* first aired as an anime in 1998 and was based off Yasuhiro Nightow's manga of the same name. In 2023, it was rebooted as *Trigun Stampede*, with Studio Orange at the helm. They drew story elements from the manga that hadn't been used in the 1998 adaptation. They also used the blend of 2D and 3D animation they'd developed for *Land of the Lustrous* and the facial expression technology from *Beastars* to create seamless action sequences and emotive characters to give viewers a never-before-seen experience. "Rather than simply tracing the original manga that started twenty-seven years ago," director Kenji Muto said, "we wanted to define the meaning of creating this work as an entertainment piece in this day and age."

Spot the Difference

Animation techniques have come a long way since they were just lines of chalk on a piece of film. Although traditional animation remains popular in many pockets of Japan, most have switched completely over to digital. Test your eyes to see what differences you can spot. *Ushio & Tora* is a good comparison between 1990s cel animation and modern digital animation. It originally ran as a series in 1992 and was rebooted in 2015. *Sailor Moon Crystal* is another example of how technology and art styles change over time while still portraying the same characters and storyline.

Many anime industry professionals were invited to Netflix's 2024 FYSEE event, including the production team from the anime-inspired show *Blue Eye Samurai*. FYSEE is an industry term that means "for your consideration." These events encourage awards show voters to support a show or film ahead of the awards presentation.

Important People

Lots of people are involved in creating an anime, from producers to editors to production coordinators. Let's highlight a couple of roles that work directly with the material from script to screen.

Director: manages the whole team; collaborates with producers, episode directors, and others; ensures production committee's satisfaction with the final product

Anime Series Director: works with the script writing team, helps lay out episode storyboards, and manages the animation team

Episode Director: oversees a single episode's flow, creative direction, and quality

Animator: works closely with the episode director to discuss flow of scenes and delivers cuts or frames of animation for episodes

Animation Director: oversees the quality of the animation and sends back any changes to the animation team

Art Director: oversees the team of background artists who create scenery

Audio Producer: coordinates with record labels to decide soundtrack music, hires composers or musicians, and works with musicians on opening and ending themes

Composer: sets the tone for the anime, from the opening and ending themes to the rest of the soundtrack

Creating an anime is a time-intensive process and requires many hands. These are just a few of the many people involved in getting an anime off the ground, animated, and recorded. The next time you watch an anime, check out the people who helped create it. Chances are, they've worked on other projects too. Some might even be responsible for your favorite show, scene, or song.

CHAPTER TWO

Creator Tools

Manga doesn't just appear overnight. It can take months or even years—in some cases, decades—to create a story that draws in an audience, has an engaging plot, and is rich enough for hours of entertainment.

Making Manga

Most people who create manga are both the author and the illustrator. In Japan, they are called mangaka. Many go to art college or even manga school. There are around one hundred manga schools throughout the country.

Entering manga competitions is the main way new creators get discovered and published. The Tezuka Award is the biggest manga award in Japan. Sponsored by Shueisha, the publisher of *Weekly Shonen Jump*, the contest dates back to 1971. There are two competitions a year. In most competitions, the judges, who work in the manga publishing industry, leave feedback. Many editors and other publishing professionals manage to find promising new artists this way.

Studying art and perfecting technique are key for anyone wanting to pursue becoming a mangaka.

First prize is a hefty two million yen, or around $18,000, as well as publication in the magazine's e-book version and an invitation to the award ceremony in Tokyo, Japan. It's an ideal launchpad for mangaka to get their careers off the ground, but it's far from the only way.

Some mangaka might submit their manuscripts directly to editors. There's a small chance editors will respond, but if the story resonates with an editor or if the editor sees enough promise in the work or mangaka, they will reach out. Editors are responsible for anything from discovering new talent, to helping mangaka develop their story to micromanaging their deadlines. An editor might help storyboard, discuss the plot, and create characters with the mangaka. The editor also talks to the target audience, taking surveys or asking questions to see reactions to the story. The editor is in charge of promoting the manga and organizing events.

Down the Pipeline

Many consider the creator of the popular series *Astro Boy*, Osamu Tezuka, to be the godfather of manga and anime. His story uses common shonen manga themes of a hero just doing his best with what he has and choosing between power and consequences when faced with conflict. Tezuka's simple art style gave Astro Boy the big eyes many have come to associate with manga. Big, expressive eyes helped Tezuka to better convey the robot character's innocence and human emotions.

The simpler design also helped Tezuka to hire assistants to make production quicker and easier. Tezuka himself had learned to draw by tracing other artists' work. He had assistants do simpler tasks that still took time, such as inking in black spaces and drawing frame outlines, while he drew more of the action shots. Together, the team could finish several hundred pages of manga a month. This system is still used in manga creation. Assistants learn every aspect of manga or anime creation while supporting mangaka, and many go on to create works of their own.

Osamu Tezuka in 1951

All Hands On Deck

If the mangaka is considered the one driving the race car, then assistants are the ones changing tires, pumping gas, and helping the mangaka cross the finish line. Because mangaka are on a tight deadline—some might be on a weekly schedule while others are on a monthly schedule—they often require assistants. Assistants' jobs vary depending on the needs of the mangaka, but generally their responsibilities include inking, shading, drawing backgrounds, and sometimes even paneling.

New manga artists might get their start as assistants to established authors. For example, Miwa Ueda, the author of shojo series *Peach Girl* and *Angel Wars*, worked as an assistant under Naoko Takeuchi, creator of *Sailor Moon*. Masashi Kishimoto's former assistant Mikio Ikemoto took up Kishimoto's legacy of continuing Naruto's story in *Boruto*. *ONE PIECE*'s creator, Eiichiro Oda, worked under many different artists at *Weekly Shonen Jump* before he found huge success with his iconic pirate series.

For mangaka, assistants are vital to keeping a project on track. According to Kyoko Kumagai, mangaka of works such as *Chocolate Vampire* and *Katayoku no Labyrinth*, "I have two series on the go at the moment—with an installment due every two weeks. Each episode is thirty pages. It would be impossible for me to come up with that much material on my own, so I always work with the help of five assistants." Kumagai always oversees their work, ensuring details remain consistent and quality remains high. Around 80 percent of all contemporary manga are drawn digitally, though some traditionalists still use pen and paper.

Make a Name

It can take time to become established as a mangaka. Artists typically start with a one-shot manga, or a short story between fifteen to sixty pages, for a magazine. If they receive enough positive attention, they might get the opportunity to expand on the one-shot or create a whole series for a magazine. This is called serialization. The magazine might be published weekly, twice a month, or monthly. Eventually, the manga will be republished as a collection in book form called tankobon.

There are three major publishers in Japan—Shueisha, which publishes *Weekly Shonen Jump*, is the largest, with

They Said What?

Manga was originally a form of media intended to appeal to children in post-World War II Japan, but because children had limited allowance money to spend, publishers needed to keep their costs low. This led to publishers printing in black and white, rather than in flashy, full-color pages like Western comics. Using less color meant artists needed to find different ways to represent visual images. Playing with word bubble shapes, text layout, frame shapes or shades, or symbols that all have their own meanings gives manga clear semiotic and symbiotic signs. People who read manga often have higher developed manga literacy and can quickly understand a story's meaning simply by looking at the art, even if they may not read at a high level—or read the original language at all.

Hajime Isayama is the creator of *Attack on Titan*, one of the best-selling manga of all time. He sold the concept based on a sixty-five-page one-shot story called *Humanity vs. Titans*.

annual sales of around $1.5 billion; Kodansha, which publishes *Weekly Shonen Magazine*; and Shogakukan, which publishes *Weekly Shonen Sunday*. There are hundreds of other publishers within Japan, including Kadokawa, Square Enix, and Fujimi Shobo.

Being a mangaka is not a typical nine-to-five job. Instead, mangaka are independent workers. If their manga is licensed by a manga publisher, they get a paycheck and royalties from tankobon. They are also paid a licensing fee if the manga is made into an anime. But often, most of the profits from anime go to the publishing companies or movie studios. "To tell the naked truth, regardless of how many people watch the film or how much the gross earnings are, not a single yen goes to the author. We are only paid an upfront license fee," Hideaki Sorachi, author of the popular series *Gintama*, said. "The amount we're paid is peanuts in comparison to the overall box office gross." That said, some authors do make it big. Eiichiro Oda, author of *ONE PIECE*, is the highest-earning manga artist of all time with a net worth of $200 million.

Coming to America

Osamu Tezuka once said that manga is a universal language. Bringing Japanese manga to English-language publishers has been huge for manga's worldwide growth. At first, major publishing houses had international divisions with just an employee or two. Foreign companies were the ones approaching the Japanese houses. They were curious about manga and its popularity. The Japanese publishing house then did its research, evaluating if there would be a financial

Shueisha's headquarters has a gallery on the first floor that is open to the public.

Founded by Stu Levy, TOKYOPOP has brought manga to fifty countries in thirty languages.

return on their investment. Sometimes, the content needed to be changed to fit the audience—for example, subjects that are considered too adult for American teenagers, such as physical relationships or excessive violence.

Translating manga is no easy task. For anime, subtitles can be added or voice tracks can be changed. But the animation can largely stay the same. Manga, on the other hand, has a limited amount of space for words. The words must also more closely match the art. This was an issue especially at first, when art was flipped to read left-to-right rather than the original right-to-left. Sometimes, art needs to be changed because of this, which artists don't like. For example, if you mirror, or flip, a panel with a samurai, you inadvertently cause the samurai to hold their sword with their left hand rather than their right. Leaving it that way is out of the question—etiquette dictated swords be worn on the left and drawn with the right hand. But changing the art is equally frustrating.

Kodansha became interested in publishing for the international market in the 1960s. Kodansha International was founded two years later. They set up offices in Tokyo, Japan; New York City, New York; and San Francisco, California. Their goal was to bring Japanese culture to places outside of Japan. They made bilingual comics for readers of both Japanese and English. Though their goal was to reach audiences outside of Japan, the company was surprised to find out how popular these bilingual comics were in Japan. Even into the 2000s, 80 percent of Kodansha Bilingual Comics readers were Japanese people who wanted to practice English.

In 1997, businessperson Stu Levy founded TOKYOPOP. The company introduced manga and anime to North America, and at its height, it was the largest manga publisher in the United States. VIZ Media brought *Weekly Shonen Jump* manga to North America in 2002. Other publishers, such as Dark Horse and Yen Press, brought additional titles over.

CHAPTER THREE

Production 101

Making a season of anime can cost millions of dollars. Much more goes into creating shows and movies than you might think! Take a peek into the behind-the-scenes secrets of anime.

How It Works

In Japan, many production companies are devoted to discovering titles and creating anime. Oftentimes anime is based on already established manga. If a production company sees potential in a certain title, it sends an offer to the manga publisher to get things rolling. Other times, the author might approach the company first. In 2020, there were more than eight hundred animation studios in Japan, with nearly seven hundred in Tokyo alone. Around three hundred anime are produced every year.

It is risky to produce anime. Aside from paying the licensing fee, the animators, musicians, voice actors, and marketing people all need to be paid as well. A single anime

Studio Pierrot is the production group behind *Naruto* and other popular anime such as *Black Clover*, *BLEACH*, and *Tokyo Ghoul*.

season can cost millions of US dollars to make. So multiple companies, such as advertisers, licensors, talent agencies, and TV stations, invest together to spread out the risk. They form a production committee to plan where each show will air, which actors or musicians to use—since some agencies also have actors or musicians signed with them—and where the show will be distributed internationally. When a studio is part of the investing team, that makes it easier to decide which animation company will take the job.

Next, a producer—and in some cases, multiple producers—is hired to oversee the entire process.

They make sure there's enough money during the project, that all the right people are hired, and that everything meets its target due dates. It takes at least two weeks to plan the whole season and around six to eight weeks to finish a single episode. The manga's creator might work closely with the animation team to make sure details are correct and true to the original story. Sometimes the animation team fills in gaps in the story or adds details the mangaka wasn't able to include in the manga.

Anime is so time-intensive to make that many studios are unable to finish a whole season before it begins airing. Often, as early episodes air, later episodes are still being completed. A studio might be working on multiple episodes at the same time.

In Japan, the broadcasting year is divided into four quarters, called *cours*. Each cour is roughly three months long. Production companies are given a time slot for when their anime can air on a TV channel during each cour. If they don't have an episode to fill that time slot, they may lose it to another company. So even if it's not an episode that advances the main plot, they need to have something ready. This sometimes results in non-canon episodes called filler. Filler episodes are more common in long-running shows such as *Naruto* or *Gintama*. *Naruto* is 41 percent filler!

One major complication with getting out new seasons of anime involves bottlenecks. Sometimes, a very popular series might take over an entire studio's production team. The studio prioritizes working on the more popular series in order to meet fan demand. A less popular show might have to wait for that team to finish the popular series first.

Let's Do It Again

Some manga get more than one adaptation. *Fruits Basket* is a story about a girl named Tohru Honda who befriends members from the Sohma clan, some of whom turn into animals of the Chinese zodiac when hugged by the opposite sex. The manga was first adapted into a single season of anime in 2001. It was so beloved by fans that it received a reboot in 2019 with three seasons that told its story to completion. The 2001 version was produced when the manga was still being published. By the time the 2019 reboot came out, the manga had already finished publication, so directors could pull from the full series.

Hiromu Arakawa's work *Fullmetal Alchemist* is another manga with more than one version. The manga was first published from 2001 to 2010. The first anime series ran from 2003 to 2004, which meant it didn't have the full manga story to pull from. In 2009 the series got a reboot by Studio Bones, the same studio that animated the 2003 version, called *Fullmetal Alchemist: Brotherhood*. It ran from 2009 to 2010, ending shortly after the manga's conclusion. Both anime are similar to the manga to a point. But once *Fullmetal Alchemist* (2003) caught up to its source material, it diverged and created its own plot and ending. *Brotherhood* was a more faithful adaptation. Although the two ended up being different stories, both anime are highly regarded.

Both *Fullmetal Alchemist* and *Fullmetal Alchemist: Brotherhood* are some of the most popular anime ever created.

Each year, fans flock to the VIZ booth at New York Comic Con.

Watch and Listen

Once an anime is complete, studios might license it to air abroad. VIZ Media, Aniplex, and Kodansha are some examples of licensors. Licensors usually take on the job of dubbing the show from the original Japanese into English, Spanish, French, or whatever other language of the area where it will be watched. Dubbing is more than just rerecording lines. Voice actors must be able to match the lip sync of the original dialogue and capture that character's personality.

Sometimes things such as expressions or turns of phrases don't translate well between languages. Other times, the translation the voice actor is given won't fit into the number of lip flaps the character has. Voice actors might talk with a script translator on how to navigate this issue, or they might improvise on the spot!

Like regular movie stars, anime voice-over actors—both Japanese and otherwise—can make names for themselves. In Japan, Kenjiro Tsuda is one example. He has voiced popular characters such as Overhaul from *My Hero Academia*, Kento Nanami from *Jujutsu Kaisen,* and Kishibe from *Chainsaw Man.* Rie Takahashi is another example of a famous voice actor. She is known as the voice of Emilia in *Re:Zero – Starting Life in Another World*, as well as for her roles in *KonoSuba: God's Blessing on This Wonderful World!, Oshi no Ko*, and *Tomo-Chan Is a Girl.*

Recognizable English-language voice actors include Christopher Sabat, who was the voice for Vegeta in *Dragon Ball Z*, All Might in *My Hero Academia*, and nearly five hundred characters across other series, games, and movies. Another is Colleen Clinkenbeard, who has voiced Monkey D. Luffy in *ONE PIECE* for more than fifteen years. She also voiced Akito Sohma in the 2019 reboot of *Fruits Basket*.

Kenjiro Tsuda has lent his voice to hundreds of anime and video game characters.

Tezuka's Curse

In 1962, Osamu Tezuka founded his own production company called Mushi. The very next year, Tezuka's company adapted his work *Astro Boy* into an anime. But in order to get ahead of his competitors, he ended up selling the rights to air his show for around ¥550,000 per episode—well under the show's value and much less than its cost to make. In comparison it cost between one and two million yen to make a single episode. This deal created a monster.

TV companies desired more low-cost shows. Many studios began saving money by hiring freelance animators desperate to work. Freelancers are expected to work long hours for low pay. Some make only thirty-eight dollars a day. They might only get paid for still frames that appear between animation, such as a shot of a house or a castle.

Although the modern anime industry is huge, wealth stays with production companies. It hasn't trickled down to the workers. The average salary for higher-level animators is only around $36,000, but some pay as low as $9,500 for new employees. Burnout and hospitalization from overwork are common. Some studios refuse to hire freelancers and insist on paying fair wages. But more companies don't.

Manga artists are under similar stress. Creators of serialized manga are expected to produce new content week after week. "Every week, after submitting my work, I'd come down with a fever and throw up anything I ate. I really did wonder, 'Can I keep this up?'" *Naruto* author Masashi Kishimoto said. "My body got more and more tired, and at one point I

Many manga artists use alcohol ink markers because they are vibrant, dry fast, and can be layered.

ended up in the hospital with an unexpected fever. . . . I just remember [the doctor] looking at a chart and saying, 'Friend, your cells are dying. You've just got to take a break.'" Kishimoto said he eventually got used to the schedule, and positive reviews from readers boosted his energy. But fans have been aware of Kishimoto working through health struggles for years.

In 2024, a blogger gathered data on 219 manga artists who had died from natural causes and found that the average male artist lived to around sixty-three. The average lifespan in Japan is eighty-five. Is manga to blame for shortened lifespans? More studies need to be done, but there is no denying that it is a grueling career path.

CHAPTER FOUR

Big Hair, Don't Care

A newcomer to anime and manga might think that the art style is singular—big eyes, cute girls, spiky hair. But there are many categories and subcategories, and each author has their own details and twists they like to use.

The Art and the Artists

Osamu Tezuka revolutionized Japanese art in multiple ways, but his idea to give Astro Boy overly large eyes is possibly the most recognizable. He continued to give this characteristic to his other characters. Using enormous eyes helps animators too. Expressive eyes can convey a character's mood, thoughts, and feelings.

Another artist who made the big-eyes look popular is Junichi Nakahara. He used large eyes in his illustrations, which appeared in fashion and shojo magazines, making the style popular among young girls and women. Eventually, his art style became the look of the entire shojo genre.

A sub-trope of anime and manga are stories that take place in schools. Many anime and manga aim to give their characters distinctive school uniforms.

Soft, pastel colors and lively shapes such as hearts and stars in the corners of pages or bouncing across the screen are also part of shojo style.

Shonen style also includes big eyes, but there is less emphasis on the pupils and tends to focus more on the overall shape. Action-oriented illustration is a big part of shonen style. *My Hero Academia* and *ONE PIECE* are great examples of distinctive shonen art. Other examples include *Akane-banashi*, *Kagurabachi*, and *Spy x Family*.

Cutesy and Demure

There are many "cute" styles that have snuck into genres or become their own form of expression. Chibi is meant to present something as small or cute. Artists exaggerate characters' features, giving them big eyes and big heads with small bodies. Originally, chibi style was used for comic relief or humor. In 1993, Naoko Takeuchi introduced a character called Chibiusa, a chibi version of Usagi, who is the main character in *Sailor Moon*. She became part of the main cast, and more chibi characters in manga followed.

The word *chibi* can also be used to describe children, people, or animals that are cute.

In 2024, Hello Kitty was worth about $8 billion. Products featuring the character range from toys and collectibles to Crocs and designer handbags.

In the 1970s, the idea of kawaii as a trend became popular. Teenagers began writing like little kids. People embraced kawaii style, dressing in a cute way. Men and women sought to seem more youthful. The ideas of adorableness and positivity were at its center. Animals with humanlike features—or people with animal characteristics, including ears and tails—became popular.

In 1974, twenty-four-year-old illustrator Yuko Shimizu was working for a sandal company called Sanrio. The company had hired many young workers to come up with more manga-inspired kawaii designs. Yuko came up with a white cat wearing a red hair bow. Hello Kitty quickly became Sanrio's mascot and the face of their most popular products. In the late 1980s, Hello Kitty finally got her own TV show. She didn't get her own manga series until 2007.

Kodomo is manga and anime aimed at young children under twelve. Characters are usually animals or children drawn with large eyes and slim bodies. Aside from *Hello Kitty*, *Anpanman*, *Doraemon*, and *Pokémon* are three famous examples of kodomo.

Realism and Horror

Not all manga and anime are cute though. Some manga exist to draw the reader in with rich art and relatable backgrounds. *Akira*, *The Way of the Househusband*, and *JoJo's Bizarre Adventure* are three popular series with art styles that lean more realistic, even if their content draws from sci-fi, slice-of-life, and adventure.

Horror manga, on the other hand, gets inspiration from ukiyo-e art and traditional Japanese folktales of vengeful demons and terrifying monsters. Junji Ito is one of the most famous horror manga writers. His works are not for young readers or the faint of heart, but he has inspired the artists who have followed in his footsteps, especially in the seinen genre.

One of a Kind

Some artists have a style so recognizable and distinctive that it is undeniably theirs. For example, *Lupin III*, created by Monkey Punch, has simple character designs but impressive action panels full of explosions, chase scenes, and exaggerated expressions. Monkey Punch took inspiration from Western icons such as Tom and Jerry and James Bond but gave them a Japanese presence.

Akira Toriyama started out drawing *Dragon Ball* using round, soft shapes and clean lines in 1984. Around this time, many other popular titles were leaning toward realism, which made Toriyama's almost bouncy art stand out even more. As the series progressed, the characters became more detailed, with harder, sharper lines. Characters had well-defined

Dragon Ball is one of the largest franchises in Japan, spanning several animated series and over twenty movies.

muscles, pointed chins, and small, pointed feet. But even as the art evolved, it remained Toriyama's individual style.

Get Inspired

Anime doesn't just inspire other anime—they also inspire cartoon styles around the world! Many cartoons have used anime as inspiration, blending Western with Japanese-style art. *Teen Titans*, *Avatar: The Last Airbender*, *Samurai Jack*, and *Powerpuff Girls* are classic examples. Because some of these shows aired alongside actual anime, sometimes the lines between the two blurred, causing confusion about what actually constituted as anime. Anime also helped Western audiences realize that cartoons weren't just for little kids. *Steven Universe* and *She-Ra: Princess of Power* were made in mind for audiences of all ages.

Mukokuseki

"Why do anime characters look white?" is a frequently asked question by both experienced fans and people new to the medium. The answer is they're not! The Japanese word *mukokuseki* means "lacking any kind of nationality characteristics," and that describes depictions of characters in manga and anime. They are popular internationally because the characters do not have distinct facial or body features that make them specifically Japanese. The fewer facial details a character has, the more easily any reader, regardless of their country of origin, can identify with them.

Others point out that Japan has long-borrowed from other cultures, and anime and manga are no exception. Still others note that Japanese artists *are* drawing Japanese characters. There is no reason for them to be drawing anything else. White readers just think they see white characters because to them, white is the default. Sometimes, white or American characters show up in manga or anime, and they often are shown as much taller, larger, or more muscular than the protagonists, with prominent chins and noses.

Some people might think that characters in *Slam Dunk* are white or another ethnicity. But they are actually Japanese students.

CHAPTER FIVE

On the Big Screen

Bringing popular manga and anime to the big screen is not new. The first feature film anime shown in Japan was *Momotarō: Umi no Shinpei*, or *Momotarō: Sacred Sailors*, in 1945. It was a propaganda film commissioned by the Japanese government.

Around the same time *Momotarō* came out, Disney was making big headways in the animation market with films such as *Snow White and the Seven Dwarves* and *Fantasia*. Business executive Hiroshi Okawa saw the studio's successes and sought to make Japan's own "Disney." In 1956, he founded Toei Douga (later Toei Animation) and became the company's president. He sent his animators to Hollywood to learn how Disney made movies. Toei's first film, released in 1958, was called *Hakujaden*, or *The White Snake Enchantress*. It was based on a Chinese folktale, and their adaptation won awards in Japan and around the world.

Toei later faced financial and labor issues, and the anime industry tanked in the early 1970s. But shows such as *Space Battleship Yamato* (*Star Blazers* in English) and *Super Dimension*

Fortress Macross (or, as it's known in America, *Macross*) made sure anime wasn't forgotten.

Getting Serious

Around the 1970s, manga for older male readers, which fell into the seinen or gekiga genres, reached its peak of popularity. These stories usually involved realistic plotlines or sports. But Katsuhiro Otomo had always loved science fiction. As a young manga artist, he spent time imagining a dystopian future setting with a touch of supernatural horror. His adult sci-fi manga *Akira* was all those things.

Akira was serialized in Kodansha's seinen biweekly *Young Magazine* starting in 1982. It was incredibly popular. The first tankobon volume was a bestseller. Then, Otomo was asked to direct the anime adaptation. There is conflicting information about how much the movie cost to make, but regardless of an exact number, Otomo knew it would be expensive to produce as he envisioned it. And Otomo was a known perfectionist.

By the late 1980s, Japan's economy had recovered, and investors were eager to put money into new projects. The Akira Production Company included big names such as Kodansha, toy company Bandai, and entertainment companies TMS Entertainment and Toho. Media companies and trade investors were also on board. It was a huge project. Otomo had to make many cuts to his original story to fit within a reasonable movie runtime. But the money and time investment were worth it.

Around the world, people still feel the movie's impact. *Akira* was so popular that for a long time, people that hadn't

Akira's color palette is as distinctive as its story. The film uses 327 different colors to tell its story, a record for the time. Fifty of the colors were brand-new, created specifically for the movie.

before been exposed to anime judged it as the standard and expectation of what anime was. Unfortunately, this meant that some people believed anime was just about sex and violence.

Let's Get Spirited Away

Possibly the most famous anime movie production company was created just a few months after *Akira*. A former Toei Animation employee, Hayao Miyazaki had made his

Nausicaä and the Valley of the Wind **is a post-apocalyptic fantasy story that follows the main character Nausicaä. The film has environmental and anti-war themes.**

directorial debut in 1979 with *Lupin III: The Castle of Cagliostro*. His next film was based on his own manga, *Nausicaä and the Valley of the Wind*, which came out in 1984. After its success, Miyazaki teamed up with producer Toshio Suzuki and director Isao Takahata to form Studio Ghibli. They animated and directed films such as *Castle in the Sky* (1986), *My Neighbor Totoro* (1988), and *Kiki's Delivery Service* (1989). But Miyazaki was deeply unhappy with the US release of *Nausicaä and the Valley of the Wind*. The 117-minute film had been cut down to 95 minutes long, and its themes of nature and humanity were tossed out in favor of a simpler action-adventure plotline. Names were changed, and the main heroine was not featured on promotional materials. The voice actors didn't even know what the movie was about.

None of Miyazaki's movies would reach American audiences again until 1996.

When the original American distributor's rights expired, Disney stepped up. They reached out to Studio Ghibli and acquired the rights to distribute their works in North America. They rerecorded an English-language version of *Nausicaä and the Valley of the Wind*, this time for the full-length film, using A-list American stars such as Patrick Stewart, Uma Thurman, and Mark Hamill. The next Studio Ghibli movie, *Princess Mononoke* (1997), was the highest-grossing Japanese film that year. It also became the first animated film to earn the Japan Academy's Picture of the Year.

Miyazaki and Ghibli continued their success with *Spirited Away*, which sold eight million tickets in its first twenty-five days at the box office. The movie made $395.6 million worldwide. It won the 2002 Golden Bear award at the Berlin International Film Festival. It also took home an Academy Award for Best Animated Feature. *Spirited Away* was the first non-English animation to win an Oscar in that category. In 2024, *The Boy and the Heron* won Best Animated Feature. Even though twenty-one years had passed since *Spirited Away*, *The Boy and the Heron* was only the second anime to ever win this award. At eighty-three years old, Miyazaki was also the oldest winner in that category.

People around the world love Studio Ghibli movies. Since 2017, Fathom Events has distributed Ghibli movies for what they call Ghiblifest. Around one thousand theaters across North America show a Studio Ghibli movie once a month between March and November. In 2023, more than $15 million in Ghiblifest tickets were sold.

The Studio Ghibli headquarters are located in a small residential neighborhood in Koganei City, Tokyo. Miyazaki lives just a few blocks away.

Ghibli movies *Ponyo*, *Howl's Moving Castle*, and *Spirited Away* are among the highest-grossing anime films of all time. *Spirited Away* held the number one spot until 2020. Then that October, *Demon Slayer: Kimetsu no Yaiba – The Movie: Mugen Train*—or *Demon Slayer: Mugen Train* in English-speaking countries—hit the big screen.

It was a risky move. The global COVID-19 pandemic had shut down movie theaters and other public spaces for months. Many studios canceled theater releases or went straight to streaming. The movie theater business had dropped around 80 percent.

Furthermore, most anime movies are stand-alone events. They do not affect the main TV show's characters or storylines or require viewers to be very familiar with past seasons or episodes. But *Mugen Train* took on the risk of being a direct sequel movie to season one of the TV anime series. It continued the story where season one had left off

Disney Anime

Besides distributing major anime properties, Disney has produced some of its own manga and anime, such as *Disney: Twisted Wonderland*, which was written by *Black Butler* creator Yana Toboso and released in 2023. That same year, Disney produced its first anime series, *Tengoku Daimakyo*, or *Heavenly Delusion*. The series was an unusual choice for the traditionally child-friendly company. The seinen manga, created by Masakazu Ishiguro, was for older readers aged thirteen to seventeen, and the anime received a TV-MA rating, for mature audiences only.

The show was hard to find too. Before Hulu and Disney+ merged in 2024, international audiences could watch *Tengoku Daimakyo* on Disney+. But for American viewers, it was on Hulu only. The show was also listed only under its Japanese name on Disney+, making some fans confused. But the people who could find it were impressed. Fans praised its animation and music.

Since 2023, Disney has been working with Kadokawa to create new original anime. Disney has also contracted with other anime licensors, steadily increasing their collection of anime on its platform.

and was plot-important for fans who wanted to watch season two.

The risk paid off. Fans flocked to the theaters. *Mugen Train* made more than $507 million worldwide, taking over the title of number one highest-grossing anime movie of all time.

It took just ten days for *Mugen Train* to reach $100 million in ticket sales in Japan.

The movie was later released as a seven-episode arc. The TV episodes followed the same plot, but also had additional, important content that fans would need to know. But the TV episodes were not aired until the following October, so the movie enjoyed a long runtime in theaters.

Anime fans looking to expand their movie library should also look out for *A Silent Voice*, *Look Back*, and *The First Slam Dunk*. All have manga as well and are good references for those who might want to compare the formats.

CHAPTER SIX

The Backstory

Anime is often based on manga, but that's not always the case. Sometimes, the original source material comes from other places. One of those places is light novels. Light novels are stories originally serialized in Japanese magazines and reprinted in bunkobon format. Bunkobon are smaller than the tankobon size manga typically come in. They're also usually thicker. Their main audience is readers who may be looking for something a little longer than manga, but not as complex as a full book or novel. When published in paperback form, they usually run around three hundred pages or less and often include illustrations both within the text and in the back of the book. *Apothecary Diaries*, *My Happy Marriage*, *Ascendance of a Bookworm*, and *Reincarnated as a Slime* are popular light novels that were later turned into manga or anime.

Some light novel authors get their start by uploading their work online to websites that encourage self-publishing and web or mobile browsing. If their stories are popular, a publisher may see them and sign them to a deal. *Sword Art*

Online, *Fate/Zero*, and *Full Metal Panic!* are a few examples of light novels that followed this path.

But this can cause some issues. Light novel authors may have written as a hobby. Their stories might not be as polished as they could be. If an editor requests revisions, authors may not have the time or ability to do them in a satisfactory way. The editor may need to do the bulk of the revisions themselves, which can be frustrating. If it sells well, the original author gets royalty payments and may even be contracted for sequels that result in more money for them and more work for the editor.

Read Your Heart Out

Some fans just like to read and watch anime and manga, but others collect books, digital media, and other collector's items. Owning a collector's edition can be a point of pride for fans, and it's also a great way to preserve physical media.

In 2022, artist Ilan Manouach published a limited edition volume that contained twenty-five years' worth of *ONE PIECE* manga. It was 21,450 pages long, with a 31.5 inch (80 cm)-wide spine. Only fifty copies existed. Each volume cost €1,900 or around $2,100 today. Half sculpture, half manga, the 37.5-pound (17-kg) work was impossible to read but looked amazing on a shelf. Every copy was sold. In 2024, one was posted on eBay with an $8,000 price tag.

Adding Words Later

Sometimes established manga or anime series get a light novel later. *Jujutsu Kaisen, Naruto,* and *Toradora!* are three examples. Doing this can bring in a new audience to a series. It also brings in more revenue, as popular light novel series can sell 600,000 to 800,000 copies a year in Japan. Light novels are not as popular in North America yet, but they're starting to catch on. If the story is good, it doesn't matter the format. People will pick them up and read.

Add to the Gaming Library

Sometimes source material for manga or anime comes from a surprising place—video games! *Pokémon* is probably the most well-known example. The first game came out in 1996. Since then, this best-selling franchise has sold more than 480 million copies and has been translated into nine different languages. Nearly sixty-five billion trading cards have been bought, sold, and traded in ninety-three countries. The success of *Pokémon* paved the way for its very own manga and anime series, which are enjoyed by over a hundred countries and regions around the world.

Star Soldier and *Super Mario Bros.* are two other popular video game examples that have inspired anime and manga extensions. On July 20, 1986, anime based on both were released on Video Home System (VHS) tapes in Japan. A Super Mario manga was serialized in Kodensha's *Comic BomBom* between 1988 and 1998 and was later turned into forty-three volumes of tankobon. The stories tied into whichever Super Mario game was out at the time.

Each volume also contained strategy tips for that game. *Kingdom Hearts, The Legend of Zelda*, and *Final Fantasy* are other games that made their way to the games-with-manga library.

The Pokémon Company is one of the largest licensors in the world. In 2023, they generated more than $11 billion through merchandise such as clothing, plushies, trading cards, toys, and more.

Choose Your Own Adventure

Visual novels are similar to light novels in that they have a novel-like structure, but with the added feature of being a role-playing game. Like games, they can be accessed through video game distribution services such as Steam, but there are specific websites dedicated to visual novels as well. These novels tell stories through digital images, animations, and sounds. The "reader" can make choices that change the storylines. They may be presented with two or three choices on the screen. Each choice leads to a new story route with more decisions. Fans can really get invested if the novel is long. Some visual novels might take only fifteen minutes to "read" through. But others can go for eighty hours or more. A good story with interesting choices can hook readers and make them feel truly immersed in the world.

Visual novels may even get so popular that they're turned into manga or anime. *Steins;Gate* and *Doki Doki Literature Club* are a few examples. Visual novels span a wide array of storylines, from dating to horror to comedy.

CameliaGirls **is a slice-of-life visual novel. It follows the story of a transfer student at an all-girls academy.**

CONCLUSION
The Final Cut

Getting manga and anime to the masses takes more than a single person armed with ink and pen. It requires writers with artistic talent, editors, publishers, translators, animators, directors, musicians, voice actors, and more. Both markets are expected to grow in the next decade. In 2023, the manga market was valued at $14 billion. By 2031, that value may reach nearly $22 billion. In 2024, anime was valued at around $30 billion and should reach nearly $75 billion by 2033. The future for Japanese media looks bright.

Whether you are a casual fan, a self-proclaimed otaku with a huge manga library, a weekend streamer, a collector, or a future artist or animator, there is a place behind the scenes to explore. (There's even a manga called *Behind the Scenes!!*) The more you know, the more you'll be able to appreciate the time and effort that go into making your favorite scenes, settings, and characters.

Creating manga and anime is hard work. Remember that there are people behind the page and screen as you binge old shows or try a new favorite. Imagine what it must be like to be the mangaka of a popular series. You can support publishers and production companies that treat their employees well. And you can let your favorites know when they've done something you love!

The more popular anime and manga becomes, the easier it will be to find it at your local bookstore and library!

GLOSSARY

adaptation: a written work that has been reworked to be a movie, TV show, or play

bilingual: fluent in two languages

canon: a work of fiction that is either created by or officially approved by the original author or developer of the world

frame: a single still image

gekiga: a style of Japanese comics aimed at adults

genre: a style of a creative work

gross: the amount of money something earns before taxes and expenses are taken out

licensing: allowing the use of copyrighted or patented material to a person or company

literacy: the ability to read and write

otaku: a person very interested in anime, manga, video games, or computers

projector: a device that plays motion picture film and projects it onto a screen

propaganda: information used to promote a political cause or point of view

reboot: to bring back a long-gone TV series or create a new one based on the older show

revenue: income made from the sale of goods and services

seinen: manga or anime whose primary audience is older men

semiotic: signs, symbols, and gestures used to communicate meaning and intent

serialize: to publish a story in regular installments, such as chapters or episodes

shojo: manga or anime whose primary audience is young girls

shonen: manga or anime whose primary audience is young boys

storyboard: rough drawings, along with scene direction and dialogue, that represent future planned shots or scenes

subtitles: captions displayed at the bottom of a viewing screen that transcribe dialogue, sounds, and narrative

symbiotic: the relationship between visual communication and meaning

tankobon: a physical book of collected manga chapters

VHS: short for *video home system*; VHS tapes are cassettes used to store and record audio and video.

SOURCE NOTES

5 "When I'm working . . . on a reader.": Yusei Matsui, *Assassination Classroom, Vol. 3*, San Francisco: VIZ Media, LLC, 2014–2018.

13 "Rather than simply . . . day and age.": Kenji Muto, quoted in Nick Valdez, "Trigun Stampede Crew Explains Why New Anime is in CG," Comicbook.com, July 19, 2022, https://comicbook.com/anime/news/trigun-stampede-anime-reboot-cg-why-explained/.

19 "I have two . . . of five assistants.": Kyoko Kumagai, quoted in "The Creation of Manga," Trends in Japan, accessed August 22, 2024, https://web-japan.org/trends/09_culture/pop110210.html.

22 "To tell the . . . box office gross.": Hideaki Sorachi, quoted in Joan Coello, "Do Manga Artists Earn Big Bucks from Film Adaptations? Gintama Author Spills the Beans," SoraNews24, November 25, 2016, https://soranews24.com/2016/11/25/do-manga-artists-earn-big-bucks-from-film-adaptations-gintama-author-spills-the-beans/.

32–33 "Every week, after . . . take a break.": Masashi Kishimoto, quoted in "How Busy is a Manga-ka's Schedule? A Day in the Life of NARUTO Author Masashi Kishimoto!," Anime Art Magazine, November 17, 2021, https://animeartmagazine.com/how-busy-is-a-manga-kas-schedule-a-day-in-the-life-of-naruto-author-masashi-kishimoto/.

SELECTED BIBLIOGRAPHY

"10 Steps to Make Your Own Manga or Comic Book." Anime Outline. Accessed September 27, 2024. https://www.animeoutline.com/steps-to-make-your-own-manga/.

Alyssa, Omak Public Library. "The Benefits of Manga and Graphic Novels." NCW Libraries, August 10, 2021. https://www.ncwlibraries.org/the-benefits-of-manga-and-graphic-novels/.

Brzeski, Patrick. "How Japanese Anime Became the World's Most Bankable Genre." *The Hollywood Reporter*, May 16, 2022. https://www.hollywoodreporter.com/business/business-news/japanese-anime-worlds-most-bankable-genre-1235146810/.

Dooley, Ben, and Hikari Hida. "Anime is Booming. So Why are Animators Living in Poverty?" *The New York Times*, February 24, 2021. Updated June 23, 2023. https://www.nytimes.com/2021/02/24/business/japan-anime.html.

Mahaseth, Harsh. "The Cultural Impact of Manga on Society." *Asian Journal of Language, Literature and Culture Studies*, January 24, 2018. https://journalajl2c.com/index.php/AJL2C/article/view/10.

Rogin, Ali, Claire Mufson, and Michael Boulter. "What's Behind the Growing Popularity of Japanese Comics and Animations in US." PBS News, May 18, 2024. https://www.pbs.org/newshour/show/whats-behind-the-growing-popularity-of-japanese-comics-and-animations-in-u-s.

Willmore, Alison. "Hayao Miyazaki Didn't Lose a Step During His Temporary Retirement." *Vulture*. Updated September 6, 2024. https://www.vulture.com/article/miyazakis-the-boy-and-the-heron-does-not-disappoint.html.

FURTHER INFORMATION

Books

Bolte, Mari. *Understanding Manga : From Fox Spirits to Fashion Icons.* Minneapolis: Twenty-First Century Books, 2026.
Learn about manga's history, who makes it, and how it's made.

Ha, Christine. *Anime and Manga.* San Diego: BrightPoint Press, 2022.
Learn how anime and manga are created and how they have impacted society.

Lawrence, Briana. *Essential Manga Guide: 50 Series Every Manga Fan Should Know.* Philadelphia: Running Press, 2024.
See recommendations and pick your next favorites series.

Lerner, Elliot. *Drawing Manga: An Illustrated Story.* San Rafael , CA: Rocky Nook, 2024.
Learn how to create manga and anime characters with your own creativity.

Mooney, Carla. *World of Manga.* San Diego: BrightPoint Press, 2024.
Explore the world of manga, from famous artists to genres and bestsellers.

Websites

British Museum: An Introduction to Manga
https://www.britishmuseum.org/blog/introduction-manga
Learn more about manga, what it is, where it came from, and how to enjoy it.

Crunchyroll: How Is Anime Made?
https://www.crunchyroll.com/news/deep-dives/2023/3/20/feature-how-is-anime-made
Learn the ins and outs of anime production.

Nashville Film Institute: What Is Anime? Everything You Need to Know
https://www.nfi.edu/what-is-anime/
What is anime? Read about the art style, history, and popularity of anime.

Nippon.com: The Evolution of the Japanese Anime Industry
https://www.nippon.com/en/features/h00043/
Trace the history of anime over the past century.

Trends in Japan: The Creation of Manga
https://web-japan.org/trends/09_culture/pop110210.html
Learn how manga has changed the world.

INDEX

ABOUT THE AUTHOR

Mari Bolte is a Korean-American writer and editor who lives in Minnesota with her family and a zoo of pets. She loves books in all formats, but has a special fondness for manhwa and manga.

PHOTO ACKNOWLEDGMENTS

Image credits: okanozdemir/Shutterstock, p. 7; Heritage Images/Contributor/Getty Images, p. 8; Mugtheboss/Wikimedia, p. 9; Faz Zaki/Shutterstock, p. 11; Natasha Campos/Stringer/Getty Images, p. 14; VALENTINE CHAPIUS/Contributor/Getty Images, p. 17; Ogiyoshisan/Wikimedia, p. 18; YOHAN BONNET/Contributor/Getty Images, p. 21; Akonnchiroll/Wikimedia, p. 23; Amy Graves/Contributor/Getty Images, p. 24; M. Faisal Riza/Shutterstock, p. 27; Bones/Album/Newscom, p. 29; Bryan Bedder/Stringer/Getty Images, p. 30; Manabu Yukawa/Wikimedia, p. 31; Tutatamafilm/Shutterstock, p. 33; Jon Hicks/Getty Images, p. 35; AdorableNinana/Shutterstock, p. 36; enchanted_fairy/Shutterstock, p. 37; cfg1978/Shutterstock, p. 39; China News Service/Contributor/Getty Images, p. 40; kuremo/Shutterstock, p. 42; Album/Fine Art Images/Newscom, p. 44; Akonnchiroll/Wikimedia, p. 46; Hiroshi-Mori-Stock/Shutterstock, p. 48; RG-vc/Shutterstock, p. 52; Zache/Wikimedia, p. 53; Hiroshi-Mori-Stock/Shutterstock, p. 55.

Cover image: Oleksandr Todorov/Getty Images